The Check-Up
and
The Fish and Chip Shop

Level 3 – Yellow

Helpful Hints for Reading at Home

The graphemes (written letters) and phonemes (units of sound) used throughout this series are aligned with Letters and Sounds. This offers a consistent approach to learning whether reading at home or in the classroom.

HERE IS A LIST OF PHONEMES FOR THIS PHASE OF LEARNING. AN EXAMPLE OF THE PRONUNCIATION CAN BE FOUND IN BRACKETS.

Phase 3			
j (jug)	v (van)	w (wet)	x (fox)
y (yellow)	z (zoo)	zz (buzz)	qu (quick)
ch (chip)	sh (shop)	th (thin/then)	ng (ring)
ai (rain)	ee (feet)	igh (night)	oa (boat)
oo (boot/look)	ar (farm)	or (for)	ur (hurt)
ow (cow)	oi (coin)	ear (dear)	air (fair)
ure (sure)	er (corner)		

HERE ARE SOME WORDS WHICH YOUR CHILD MAY FIND TRICKY.

Phase 3 Tricky Words			
he	you	she	they
we	all	me	are
be	my	was	her

TOP TIPS FOR HELPING YOUR CHILD TO READ:

- Allow children time to break down unfamiliar words into units of sound and then encourage children to string these sounds together to create the word.
- Encourage your child to point out any focus phonics when they are used.
- Read through the book more than once to grow confidence.
- Ask simple questions about the text to assess understanding.
- Encourage children to use illustrations as prompts.

This book focuses on the phonemes /qu/, /ch/ and /sh/ and is a yellow level 3 book band.

The Check-Up
and
The Fish and Chip Shop

Written by
Georgie Tennant

Illustrated by
Drue Rintoul

Can you say this sound and draw it with your finger?

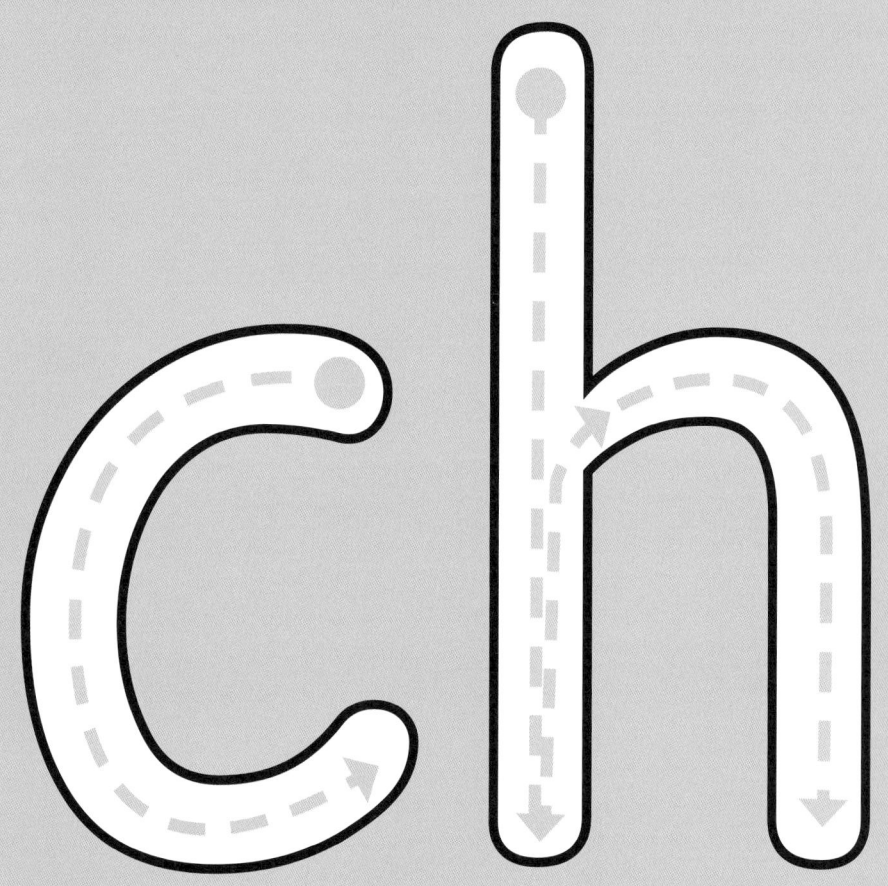

The Check-Up

Written by
Georgie Tennant

Illustrated by
Drue Rintoul

Chez and Chuck go to a check-up.
It will be fun.

Chez, Chuck and Mum sit. Max has a lot to do.

Chez is fed up. She gets up on the box.

Chez yells. She has hit her chin.
Mum gets Chez to sit.

Chuck is fed up. He gets up to run.

Zigzag. Bash! Quick, Mum! Chuck is in the bin!

Chuck yells. He has hit his shin. Such a big fuss.

Max tells Mum to get Chez and Chuck to him.

Max checks the gash. He will fix it.

Max checks the bash. He will fix it.

Max tells Chez and Chuck to sip the red liquid.

Mum sips the hot liquid.
The check-up was not fun!

Can you say this sound and draw it with your finger?

The Fish and Chip Shop

Written by
Georgie Tennant

Illustrated by
Drue Rintoul

Chaz is in his fish shop. He gets the bucket of fish.

Chaz tips the fish into the liquid.
Such a mess!

Chaz checks the fish. He gets such a shock. It is big.

Chuck tells Mum he will get fish and chips.

Mum gets the cash. Chuck will rush to the chip shop.

Chuck is at the fish and chip shop.
It is shut.

Chaz lets Chuck in. Gosh! Such a big fish!

Chaz gets a big dish. It will not fit!

Chaz chops the fish up. It fits!

The shop is not shut. They all get in.

They all get a bit of the big fish.
Yum yum!

Chuck gets the fish and chips back to Mum. Yum yum!

©2022 **BookLife Publishing Ltd.**
King's Lynn, Norfolk, PE30 4LS, UK

ISBN 978-1-80155-472-5
All rights reserved. Printed in Poland.
A catalogue record for this book is available from the British Library.

The Check-Up & The Fish and Chip Shop
Written by Georgie Tennant
Illustrated by Drue Rintoul

An Introduction to BookLife Readers...

Our Readers have been specifically created in line with the London Institute of Education's approach to book banding and are phonetically decodable and ordered to support each phase of Letters and Sounds.

Each book has been created to provide the best possible reading and learning experience. Our aim is to share our love of books with children, providing both emerging readers and prolific page-turners with beautiful books that are guaranteed to provoke interest and learning, regardless of ability.

BOOK BAND GRADED using the Institute of Education's approach to levelling.

PHONETICALLY DECODABLE supporting each phase of Letters and Sounds.

EXERCISES AND QUESTIONS to offer reinforcement and to ascertain comprehension.

BEAUTIFULLY ILLUSTRATED to inspire and provoke engagement, providing a variety of styles for the reader to enjoy whilst reading through the series.

AUTHOR INSIGHT:
GEORGIE TENNANT

Georgie Tennant is a freelance writer who has written multiple stories for BookLife Publishing. She always knew she would be a writer as she used to present her school teachers with lengthy stories and poems for them to enjoy! Her two sons provide plenty of entertaining material for her writing, which usually appears on her blog or in the local newspaper as the 'Thought for the Week'. When she isn't writing she is working as a part-time secondary school English teacher, where she has the pleasure of inspiring slightly bigger children with the joy of reading good stories. She hopes to write good stories for them one day too.

This book focuses on the phonemes /qu/, /ch/ and /sh/ and is a yellow level 3 book band.